Runes for Mindfulness

M J MEREDITH

Runes for Mindfulness

CONTENTS

Section 1: How to Use This Pocket Companion 1

Section 2: Mindfulness Basics 4

Section 3: Mindfulness in Action 7

Section 4: Elder Futhark Quick Reference Guide 12

Section 5: Rune Meditation Scripts – Elder Futhark 17

Section 6: Detailed Rune Rituals 68

Section 7: Quick Prompt Reference Guide 72

Section 8: Final Thoughts 76

Section 9: Further Reading/
Other Resources 78

Copyright © 2025 by M J Meredith & Celtic Stag
All rights reserved. No part of this book may be reproduced in any manner whatsoever without written permission except in the case of brief quotations embodied in critical articles and reviews.
First Printing, 2025

Section 1: How to Use This Pocket Companion

As the title suggests this guide is a companion to the full reference book Runes For Mindfulness: A Simple Guide to Inner Peace. This companion is designed to be flexible, practical, and easy to weave into even the busiest schedule. There's no "right" way to use it, only what works best for you.

Option 1: Let Intuition Lead

Open the companion at random and allow the rune you land on to guide your reflection. Sometimes the message you most need is the one you weren't expecting. (Section 5 Rune Meditation Scripts – Elder Futhark)

Option 2: Choose with Intention

If you're facing a specific challenge. A stressful meeting, a tight deadline, or a difficult decision, select the rune that aligns with the guidance or energy you need most. (Section 4 Quick Reference Guide)

Suggested Daily or Weekly Practices

- **Morning Reset:** Spend 3–5 minutes with a rune before your day begins. Reflect on its meaning, use the quick affirmation, and set your intention.
- **De-stress Pause:** Take a moment with a rune as a grounding exercise to help you through those stressful moments.
- **End-of-Day Reflection:** Revisit the rune of the day and jot down how its message showed up in your day, choices, or interactions.

Even just a few mindful minutes can provide clarity, reduce stress, and help you approach work with greater calm and focus. The key is consistency. Small pauses add up to meaningful shifts in balance and perspective. Go to Section 6 for more detailed Runic Rituals

Section 2: Mindfulness Basics

Mindfulness 101

At its core, mindfulness is the practice of focusing one's awareness on the present moment, while calmly acknowledging and accepting thoughts, feelings, and bodily sensations. It's a way of grounding ourselves in the *now*, free from the distractions of past regrets or future anxieties.

The 20th century saw the development of Mindfulness-Based Stress Reduction (MBSR) programs that have proven effective in reducing anxiety, depression, and stress.

In our fast-paced, hyper-connected world, it offers a reprieve, a way to step back from the noise and reconnect with ourselves.

When practised regularly, mindfulness helps us observe our thoughts and emotions without being swept away by them. This creates space for calm, clarity, and a sense of control.

In Brief: Mindfulness-Based Practices

- **Reduce Stress** and has been shown to reduce cortisol.
- **Enhance Focus and Attention** through training the mind to remain present, mindfulness helps improve concentration and productivity.
- **Aid with Emotional Regulation** by encouraging self-awareness, helping us respond thoughtfully rather than react impulsively.
- **Improve Mental Health** Studies show regular mindfulness practice is linked to reduced symptoms of anxiety and depression, and improved overall wellbeing.
- **Create Physical Health Benefits** that research suggests mindfulness can lower blood pressure, support immune health, and improve sleep quality.

Mindfulness Is a Lifelong Journey

Mindfulness is not a destination but an ongoing practice. A daily return to presence, awareness, and self-reflection. The runes provide a symbolic structure for this journey, offering evolving insights as you grow and change.

Mindfulness and Runes

At their heart Runic symbols become a visual tool that your mind can anchor too. Elder Futhark runes offer rich symbolism and meaning that invites deeper self-reflection.

Each rune becomes a moment of pause, a chance to breathe, to reflect, to realign. By working with runes in a mindful way, you can access new layers of awareness, peace, and personal empowerment.

Section 3: Mindfulness in Action

Quick "How To" of Mindfulness Practices

Rune Meditation (3-5+ Minutes)

- **Claim your space**: Find a quiet, comfortable space. Set soft lighting or use natural light
- **Session intention:** Decide if you want to use meaningful objects or just your mind. Clarify your intention for the session. Choose your rune (intuitively, deliberately, or by casting)
- **Be aware of your breath:** Use calming breath technique (try 4-7-8 breathing).
- **Anchor in the now:** Visualise or hold your rune, contemplate its symbolism (Optional: Repeat the rune's name as a mantra). Sit with the rune's energy; allow thoughts and

feelings. Gradually return to awareness before ending.
- **Reflection:** Journal any insights or reflections. Keep the rune visible if it offers ongoing guidance

Create Your Runic Bubble (1 Minute):

- **Pause & Breathe** - Take a slow, deep breath in through your nose, hold it for a moment, then exhale gently and fully. Feel your shoulders drop as tension melts away.
- **Choose a Rune** - If you carry your runes, pull one out now. If not, simply recall a rune that resonates with your current mood or need or picture one in your mind's eye. When in doubt, call on **Algiz (ᛉ)**, the rune of protection and calm.
- **Visualise & Focus** - Inhale deeply and see the rune glowing softly in your mind, its shape forming a protective bubble around you. A shield of serenity and strength.
- **Mantra & Meaning** - Silently repeat the rune's name. For example, "Algiz, Algiz, Algiz" or focus on a key word linked to its

energy, like "protection," "strength," or "calm."
- **Exhale & Release** As you breathe out, imagine stress and distractions flowing out of your body, leaving you centred and grounded. Carry this bubble of calm with you as you move forward.

With just sixty seconds, you've created your own sanctuary. A quick reset to reconnect with the present and find peace in the chaos.

A Gentle Reminder

It's natural for your mind to wander, even in this brief practice. When it does, simply acknowledge the distraction without judgement and gently return your focus to the rune and your breath. Each return strengthens your calm.

Other Breathing Techniques

Runic Breath Alignment

This simple technique uses your breath to embody the essence of a rune.

How it works:

- On your **inhale**, visualise the shape and symbolism of a chosen rune.
- On your **exhale**, release tension, distractions, or resistance. Allowing the rune's energy to settle within you.

Rhythmic Breathing with Rune Chanting

This technique adds a rhythmic structure to your breath, while engaging with the sound and vibration of a rune's name.

The 4-4-4-4 Box Breath Method:

- Inhale for 4 counts
- Hold for 4 counts
- Exhale for 4 counts
- Hold for 4 counts

As you move through each phase, silently chant or internally repeat the rune's name. Focus on its meaning and let that energy colour your breath.

The Three-Rune Breath

This short sequence is a powerful emotional re-set, perfect for those moments when you're feeling overwhelmed, reactive, or scattered.

The practice:

- **First breath – Inhale:** Visualise **Laguz**, the rune of water, representing flow and emotional release. Let your breath wash over you like a tide.
- **Second breath – Hold:** Visualise **Jera**, the rune of cycles and patience. Feel into the pause, a moment of alignment with natural timing.
- **Third breath – Exhale:** Visualise **Dagaz**, the rune of breakthrough and transformation. Release your breath with intention, imagining a new beginning.

Section 4: Elder Futhark Quick Reference Guide

Rune	Keywords	Rune	Keywords
Fehu	Abundance and Beginnings **Theme:** Prosperity, Possessions, New Beginnings	Kenaz	Illumination and Creativity **Theme:** Torch, inner light, clarity
Uruz	Strength and Vitality **Theme:** Physical strength, resilience, health	Raidho	Journey and Rhythm **Theme:** Travel, life path, cosmic order
Thurisaz	Boundaries and Protection **Theme:** Defence, powerful transformation, warning	Gebo	Gift and Connection **Theme:** Generosity, balance, partnership
Anuz	Wisdom and Communication **Theme:** Divine message, expression, inspiration	Wunjo	Joy and Harmony **Theme:** Bliss, comfort, shared happiness

Rune	Keywords	Rune	Keywords
Hagalaz	Embracing the Storm **Theme:** Disruption, transformation, necessary change	Eihwaz	Strength of the Yew **Theme:** Defence, transformation, resilience
Nauthiz	Necessity and Endurance **Theme:** Need, resistance, discipline	Perthro	Mystery and Destiny **Theme:** Fate, secrets, chance
Isa	Stillness and Focus **Theme:** Ice, stillness, clarity	Algiz	Sacred Protection **Theme:** Defence, boundaries, divine connection
Jera	Cycles of Completion **Theme:** Harvest, reward, natural cycles	Sowilo	The Inner Sun **Theme:** Victory, clarity, illumination

Rune	Keywords	Rune	Keywords
Tiwaz	The Courage to Act **Theme:** Honour, justice, self-sacrifice	Laguz	Flow and Intuition **Theme:** Water, emotion, inner knowing
Berkano	Gentle Growth **Theme:** Nurture, birth, healing	Ingwaz	Sacred Space Within **Theme:** Fertility, rest, potential
Ehwaz	Moving Forward Together **Theme:** Partnership, movement, progress	Othala	Legacy and Belonging **Theme:** Inheritance, ancestry, home
Mannaz	Knowing the Self **Theme:** Humanity, community, higher mind	Dagaz	The Moment of Awakening **Theme:** Breakthrough, new beginnings, enlightenment
Odin's Rune	The Sacred Unknown (aka Wyrd or Blank Rune) **Theme:** Trust, fate, divine will		

Notes:

Section 5: Rune Meditation Scripts – Elder Futhark

Fehu

FEHU - Abundance and Beginnings

Theme: Prosperity, Possessions, New Beginnings

Meditation Script:

Find a comfortable seated position. Close your eyes gently.

Breathe in deeply... and breathe out slowly.

Bring your awareness to the energy stirring within you.

Visualise the rune Fehu glowing softly in a golden hue.

Let it represent abundance. Not just material wealth, but also love, experience, and opportunity.

Repeat silently: *"I welcome prosperity. I honour what I have and what is yet to come."*

Breathe in the possibility of new beginnings.

With each breath, feel yourself grounded and open to growth.

When you're ready, return your awareness to the present.

Personal Notes:

Uruz

URUZ - Strength and Vitality

Theme: Physical strength, resilience, health

Meditation Script:

Find stillness and let your breath become slow and steady.

Visualise Uruz, shaped like the curved horns of ancient aurochs.

Feel strength rising from deep within your bones, muscles, and will.

Repeat silently: *"I embody strength. I am resilient. I am alive."*

Let this energy fill you.

Sit with it and honour your body.

Return to the present with gratitude.

Personal Notes:

Thurisaz

THURISAZ - Boundaries and Protection

Theme: Defence, powerful transformation, warning

Meditation Script:

Draw a breath in through your nose... and out through your mouth.
Visualise Thurisaz, bright and bold like a lightning bolt.
Feel its protective shield forming around you.
Reflect on where you need boundaries in your life.
Repeat silently: *"I protect my space. I honour my strength. I am ready for transformation."*
Anchor this intention with your breath.
Remain here until you feel steady.

Personal Notes:

Anuz

ANSUZ – Wisdom and Communication

Theme: Divine message, expression, inspiration

Meditation Script:

Relax your shoulders.

Visualise Ansuz, the rune of divine breath and inspired speech.

Imagine wind moving through trees, whispers of ancient knowledge.

Repeat silently: *"I speak truth. I listen deeply. I am guided by wisdom."*

Stay here. Listen. Receive.

Feel your throat and heart gently align.

Carry this awareness into your day.

Personal Notes:

Raidho

RAIDHO – Journey and Rhythm

Theme: Travel, life path, cosmic order

Meditation Script:

Settle in and tune to the rhythm of your breath. Inhaling... exhaling.
Visualise Raidho, a wheel turning with purpose.
See your path unfolding before you, one step at a time.
Repeat silently: *"I trust the journey. I walk with purpose and flow."*
Let this rhythm move through you.
Return when you're ready, steady and sure.

Personal Notes:

Kenaz

KENAZ – Illumination and Creativity

Theme: Torch, inner light, clarity

Meditation Script:

Take a breath. Visualise Kenaz, a flame in the darkness.
Let it represent your insight and creative spark.
Repeat silently: *"My light reveals. I see. I create."*
Let this flame burn away confusion.
Stay with the warmth and clarity it brings.
Return carrying this light with you.

Personal Notes:

GEBO – Gift and Connection

Theme: Generosity, balance, partnership

Meditation Script:

Breathe in deeply. Visualise the X-shape of Gebo.

See it as a meeting point. Giving and receiving.

Repeat silently: *"I give with grace. I receive with gratitude. I am connected."*

Open your heart to reciprocity.

Feel the strength in shared energy.

Bring this harmony into your awareness.

Personal Notes:

Wunjo

WUNJO – Joy and Harmony

Theme: Bliss, comfort, shared happiness

Meditation Script:

Smile softly. Deepen your breath.

Visualise Wunjo, a flag of joy waving freely.

Feel warmth spread through your chest.

Repeat silently: *"Joy is within me. I invite harmony. I share happiness."*

Feel light and uplifted.

Return with this brightness held gently inside you.

Personal Notes:

HAGALAZ – Embracing the Storm

Theme: Disruption, transformation, necessary change

Meditation Script:

Find stillness. Settle into your breath. Inhale deeply... exhale slowly.

Visualise a storm gathering Not to fear, but to respect.

See Hagalaz appear like hail, sudden and sharp.

This rune reminds you that upheaval is a doorway to growth.

Ask yourself: *"What storm am I resisting? What must break for new patterns to emerge?"*

Let Hagalaz clear your fears. Feel tension release.

Repeat silently: *"This is not destruction without purpose, it's shaking loose what no longer serves you."*

Breathe out doubt. Breathe in strength.

You stand in the eye of your own transformation.

Personal Notes:

NAUTHIZ – Necessity and Endurance

Nauthiz

Theme: Need, resistance, discipline

Meditation Script:

Breathe in slowly. Hold. Exhale gently.

Visualise Nauthiz, a symbol of challenge and friction.

Discomfort may rise; that's okay.

Ask: *What do I truly need? Where am I called to endure?*

Nauthiz offers growth through persistence.

Sit with the tension and let it soften as you breathe.

Repeat silently: *"I choose patience and grace with each breath."*

Know your strength is being tempered for the path ahead.

Personal Notes:

ISA – Stillness and Focus

Theme: Ice, stillness, clarity
Meditation Script:

Isa Close your eyes and breathe deeply.

Visualise a still, frozen lake, clear, silent, pure.
See Isa suspended in ice, simple, straight, steady.
Let its stillness calm your mind.
Allow thoughts to settle like snowflakes on ice.
Repeat silently: *"In stillness, I find clarity. I am centred. I am calm."*
Stay with the quiet. There's no need to rush.
Carry this stillness into your day.

Personal Notes:

JERA – Cycles of Completion

Theme: Harvest, reward, natural cycles

Meditation Script:

Slow your breath. Tune into your body's rhythm.

Visualise Jera glowing, a symbol of patient reward.

Ask: *"What am I growing? What stage am I in? Planting, nurturing, harvesting?*

There is no rushing Jera. Trust the cycle.

Breathe in this knowing. Celebrate what is complete.

Make peace with what is yet to come.

Let this rune ground you in natural timing.

Personal Notes:

Eihwaz

EIHWAZ – Strength of the Yew

Theme: Defence, transformation, resilience

Meditation Script:

Let your breath root you, inhale through your nose, exhale through your mouth.

Visualise Eihwaz, tall and protective like the ancient yew tree.

Ask: *What am I being asked to face? Where must I hold my ground?*

Feel resilience fortify your spine, rooted deep and reaching high.

With each breath, know you are protected.

You are both shield and seeker.

Personal Notes:

Perthro

PERTHRO – Mystery and Destiny

Theme: Fate, secrets, chance
Meditation Script:

Breathe into the unknown. Release control.

Visualise Perthro, a cup ready to be cast, its outcome unseen.

Ask: *What mystery is unfolding? Can I surrender to not knowing?*

Embrace the gamble, trust life's roll of the dice.

Inhale curiosity. Exhale control.

Let the mystery deepen your awareness.

There is magic in uncertainty.

Personal Notes:

Algiz

ALGIZ – Sacred Protection

Theme: Defence, boundaries, divine connection

Meditation Script:

Close your eyes and take a breath.

Visualise a great antlered guardian rising before you, Algiz, sacred protection.

Ask: *Where do I need shielding? What boundary must strengthen?*

Feel its protective aura surrounding you.

Its energy is fierce yet gentle, preserving what matters.

With each breath, feel empowered.

You are safe, supported, connected to something greater.

Personal Notes:

SOWILO – The Inner Sun

Sowilo

Theme: Victory, clarity, illumination

Meditation Script:

Breathe in sunlight. Let it fill your chest.

Visualise Sowilo rising like the morning sun, warmth cutting through confusion.

Ask: *Where do I need clarity? What part of me is ready to shine?*

Let go of darkness with each breath.

Let your inner sun rise.

You are radiant, enough, moving forward.

Personal Notes:

Tiwaz

TIWAZ – The Courage to Act

Theme: Honour, justice, self-sacrifice

Meditation Script:

Inhale courage. Exhale truth.
Visualise Tiwaz, the upright spear of the warrior's rune.
Ask: *Where must I take a stand? What value will I uphold at any cost?*
Honour is not always easy but always right.
Feel your resolve anchor here.
Stand tall. Speak with integrity.
Call forth your inner warrior of purpose.

Personal Notes:

BERKANO – Gentle Growth

Berkano

Theme: Nurture, birth, healing

Meditation Script:

Breathe gently, like a seedling stretching toward light.

Visualise Berkano, the birch rune, soft and maternal.

Ask: *What needs nurturing? Where can I show compassion to myself?*

Let Berkano wrap around your heart like warm earth around roots.

You are growing. Healing is happening, even if unseen.

Each breath is an act of self-care. You are enough.

Personal Notes:

EHWAZ – Moving Forward Together

Theme: Partnership, movement, progress

Meditation Script:

Inhale trust. Exhale fear.

Visualise Ehwaz, two horses side by side, a symbol of partnership.

Ask: *Where am I called to move forward? Who walks beside me?*

Progress need not be lonely.

With each breath, match your pace to your purpose.

Together, you can move toward what's next.

Personal Notes:

MANNAZ – Knowing the Self

Theme: Humanity, community, higher mind

Meditation Script:

Close your eyes and return to your breath.

Inhale identity. Exhale illusion.

Visualise Mannaz, the open, symmetrical human rune.

Ask: *Who am I becoming? How do I connect as my true self?*

Look inward and outward with care.

You are part of a larger pattern. Your truth matters.

Align with your highest self with each breath.

Personal Notes:

Laguz

LAGUZ – Flow and Intuition

Theme: Water, emotion, inner knowing

Meditation Script:

Float into stillness. Breathe in... breathe out.

Visualise Laguz rippling like water flowing through you.

Ask: *"Where am I resisting flow? What truths lie beneath the surface?"*

Trust your emotions. Dive deeper.

Feel your breath like waves, steady, fluid, unforced.

Let go. Trust the current. You are carried.

Personal Notes:

INGWAZ – Sacred Space Within

Theme: Fertility, rest, potential

Meditation Script:

Inhale deeply. Settle into quiet.
Visualise Ingwaz, a sacred seed enclosed and whole.
Ask: *What is gestating within me? What dream needs space and patience?*
Not all progress is visible.
Some growth happens in silence and dark.
Honor your incubation with every breath. You are becoming.

Personal Notes:

OTHALA – Legacy and Belonging

Theme: Inheritance, ancestry, home

Meditation Script:

Breathe deeply. Feel the roots beneath your feet.
Visualise Othala, ancient stone, firm and enduring.
Ask: *What legacy do I carry? Where do I truly belong?*
Connect with lineage, history, and chosen family.
Let Othala anchor you in place and purpose.
Each breath brings you home to yourself.

Personal Notes:

DAGAZ

– The Moment of Awakening

Theme: Breakthrough, new beginnings, enlightenment

Meditation Script:

Breathe in the dawn. Exhale the night.

Visualise Dagaz glowing on the horizon, the threshold of dark and light.

Ask: *What awakening is ready to break through? Where is light returning?*

This rune is hope and joy.

Feel your consciousness expand with every breath.

Step into the new. Let it begin.

Personal Notes:

ODIN'S RUNE – The Sacred Unknown (aka Wyrd or Blank Rune)

Odin's Rune

Theme: Trust, fate, divine will

Meditation Script:

Breathe into silence. No symbol appears, only space.

This is Odin's Rune, the unknowable void.

Ask: *Can I surrender to mystery? Am I willing to release the need for answers?*

Sit in this sacred pause, no meaning to grasp, no sign to decipher.

Just breathe. Just being.

Here, anything is possible. You are ready.

Personal Notes:

Section 6: Detailed Rune Rituals

Morning Rune Ritual: Setting the Tone for the Day

Begin your day by drawing or intuitively selecting a rune.

- Spend a few moments contemplating its meaning.
- Ask yourself: *What quality or message is this rune offering me today?*
- Take three slow, intentional breaths while holding the rune (physically or in your mind).
- If you like, write a short affirmation inspired by the rune's energy. For example:
    - With **Sowilo** , you might say: *"Today, I shine with clarity and strength."*

This simple ritual encourages mindfulness and sets an intentional tone before the day sweeps you up.

Rune Touchstone: A Grounding Practice for Busy Minds

Select a rune that feels grounding or protective, and carry it with you. Like a rune symbol on a pendant, rune stone in your pocket, or as a small card in your wallet.

- During the day, when you feel scattered, anxious or distracted, pause.
- Hold the rune in your hand (or bring it to mind) and take one deep breath in and out.
- Repeat a calming phrase that resonates with the rune's energy. For example:
    - *"With Isa, I find stillness."*
    - *"With Perthro, I accept what I cannot control."*

This micro-ritual can take as little as 30 seconds but can powerfully recenter you during challenging moments.

Evening Rune Release: Letting Go of the Day

Before bed, take a moment to close the day with intention.

- Choose a rune and reflect: *What lesson did I learn today?*
- Write a brief note in your journal or simply speak it aloud, focusing on something you're grateful for or something you're ready to let go of.
- With your eyes closed, take three deep breaths, visualising the rune helping you dissolve the day's stress.
- Picture the rune gently fading into the background, carrying away tension as you prepare for rest.

This ritual can help you sleep more peacefully and bring closure to the emotional and mental clutter of the day.

These rituals are not about perfection, they're about presence. Whether you spend one minute or ten, each moment spent connecting with the runes becomes a thread in your own personal tapestry of mindfulness.

Section 7: Quick Prompt Reference Guide

Rune	Prompt	Rune	Prompt
Fehu	"I welcome prosperity. I honour what I have and what is yet to come."	Kenaz	"I trust the journey. I walk with purpose and flow."
Uruz	"I embody strength. I am resilient. I am alive."	Raidho	"My light reveals. I see. I create."
Thurisaz	"I embody strength. I am resilient. I am alive."	Gebo	"I give with grace. I receive with gratitude. I am connected."
Anuz	"I speak the truth. I listen deeply. I am guided by wisdom."	Wunjo	"Joy is within me. I invite harmony. I share happiness."

Rune	Prompt	Rune	Prompt
Hagalaz	"This is not destruction without purpose, it's shaking loose what no longer	Eihwaz	What am I being asked to face? Where must I hold my ground?
Nauthiz	"I choose patience and grace with each breath."	Perthro	What mystery is unfolding? Can I surrender to not knowing?
Isa	"In stillness, I find clarity. I am centred. I am calm."	Algiz	Where do I need shielding? What boundary must strengthen?
Jera	"What am I growing? What stage am I in? Planting, nurturing, harvesting?"	Sowilo	Where do I need clarity? What part of me is ready to shine?

Rune	Prompt	Rune	Prompt
Tiwaz	"Where must I take a stand? What value will I uphold at any cost?"	Laguz	"Where am I resisting flow? What truths lie beneath the surface?"
Berkano	"What needs nurturing? Where can I show compassion to myself?"	Ingwaz	What is gestating within me? What dream needs space and patience?
Ehwaz	Where am I called to move forward? Who walks beside me?	Othala	What legacy do I carry? Where do I truly belong?
Mannaz	Who am I becoming? How do I connect as my true self?	Dagaz	What awakening is ready to break through? Where is light returning?
Odin's Rune	Can I surrender to mystery? Am I willing to release the need for answers?		

Section 8: Final Thoughts

Breath and runes share a quiet magic. Each invisible but deeply felt. Pairing the two is not about adding complexity, but about amplifying simplicity. You don't need hours or incense or elaborate rituals.

Just a breath, a symbol, and your attention.

This pocket guide works beautifully on its own, but if you'd like to go deeper into history, mythology, and psychology of runes, read the main guide. Visit www.celticstaggiftware.com

Message from the Author

Dear Reader,

Thank you for walking this path with me. Exploring the world of runes through the lens of mindfulness. I hope the insights shared throughout these pages have offered you a clearer compass for navigating life's challenges with greater awareness, peace, and purpose.

This practice is yours now and uniquely yours to shape. There is no single 'right' way to connect with the runes. Let your intuition guide you, and don't be afraid to explore what feels true to your heart.

The journey doesn't end here. With each breath, each mindful moment, may you find serenity and strength in equal measure.

With warmth and gratitude,

MJ

Section 9: Further Reading/Other Resources

If you enjoyed this book, here are some ways to continue your journey with me.

Runes for Mindfulness: A Simple Guide to Inner Peace
This book expands on the concepts in this pocket guide, taking you deeper into the history, symbolism, and practical use of Elder Futhark runes as tools for self-awareness, focus, and calm in a busy world.

Runes for Mindfulness Journal
A companion to *Runes for Mindfulness*, this journal provides guided prompts, rune reflections, and writing space to help you integrate mindfulness practices into daily life.

The Pocket Rune Rest: Mindfulness for Business & Balance A simple, practical reset for small business owners. It is a Mindfulness tool you can use in just minutes to reduce stress and refocus.

Runic Connections, A Practical Handbook to Creating Binding Runes: explores the timeless wisdom of the Elder Futhark through the lens of mindfulness, symbolism, and self-awareness. Blending ancient knowledge with modern reflection, this book helps readers understand how runes can guide personal growth, strengthen intuition, and create a deeper connection between mind, spirit, and everyday life.

Stop Defending: An Emotional Self-Defence Guide

A practical handbook for handling emotional bullying and unhealthy dynamics, this guide teaches you how to stop falling into defensiveness and instead respond with strength, clarity, and composure. It includes strategies, worksheets, and practical exercises for building emotional resilience.

How I Failed at Network Marketing to Succeed in Life

Part memoir, part life lesson, this book shares my journey through the ups and downs of network marketing. It's about finding success beyond failure—how embracing mistakes, learning from setbacks, and staying true to yourself can ultimately lead to a more authentic and fulfilling life.

www.ingramcontent.com/pod-product-compliance
Lightning Source LLC
Chambersburg PA
CBHW020545080526
44583CB00013B/1007